100 DAYS OF JOURNALING

Welcome to your 100 days of journaling!

Each day has a different prompt for you to journal about. Some may be easy to write but other days may require some more deep thinking and self-reflection. The aim is for you to become more self—aware, know yourself better and fall in love with the process of journaling.

There are no rules to how you answer the prompts. You can draw, create mind-maps, lists, etc. Feel free to take creative licence, but if you just want to write the answers that's okay too. Make sure you dedicate your full attention when you journal and be honest.

Other than that, enjoy your 100 days of journaling! I hope you learn something new about yourself.

LOVENDU

BEFORE YOU START...

Use this space to describe yourself. What do you like? Do not like? Want to achieve or your dreams? How do you perceive yourself? Then write what you're hoping to get out of this journaling experience.

DAY ONE

What does your ideal day look like?

DAY TWO

What parts of your life are you happy with?

DAY THREE

What do you think is your biggest weakness? How can you work on improving this?

DAY FOUR

What does happiness mean to you?

DAY FIVE

Talk about a time you helped someone.

DAY SIX

Who inspires you?

DAY SEVEN

List two memories you cherish the most.

DAY EIGHT

What are your biggest strengths?

DAY NINE

What does your dream job look like?

DAY TEN

What are your favourite inspirational quotes?

DAY ELEVEN

What inspires you in life?

DAY TWELVE

When do you feel most relaxed?

DAY THIRTEEN

Currently, what are your three biggest goals?

DAY FOURTEEN

What is going well in your life right now?

DAY FIFTEEN

When are you happiest?

DAY SIXTEEN

What are your favourite films?

DAY SEVENTEEN

If you could talk to your future self, what would you say?

DAY EIGHTEEN

Do you have any regrets?

DAY NINETEEN

How are you practicing self-care daily?

DAY TWENTY

What are your favourite books and why?

DAY TWENTY-ONE

List three of your fears and the reason behind them?

DAY TWENTY-TWO

How are you feeling today?

DAY TWENTY-THREE

What is the last compliment you received? And what was the last compliment you gave?

DAY TWENTY-FOUR

When was the last time you have shown kindness to a stranger?

DAY TWENTY-FIVE

How are you moving towards your goals?

DAY TWENTY-SIX

What does your dream home look like?

DAY TWENTY-SEVEN

If you could talk to your future self, what would you say?

DAY TWENTY-EIGHT

What do you wish you could tell someone, but you are too afraid?

DAY TWENTY-NINE

What is your favourite thing to do to treat yourself?

DAY THIRTY

List five things you can do for yourself to show yourself love?

DAY THIRTY-ONE

How can you improve time management and be more productive?

DAY THIRTY-TWO

What is your morning routine? Does it support your dream life?

DAY THIRTY-THREE

What traits do you admire in someone?

DAY THIRTY-FOUR

What parts of your life do you want to work on?

DAY THIRTY-FIVE

Describe your biggest supporter and why they believe in you.

DAY THIRTY-SIX

Where is your favourite place you have travelled to.

DAY THIRTY-SEVEN

Try to think of a life-changing moment, what happened then?

DAY THIRTY-EIGHT

Describe your favourite foods.

DAY THIRTY-NINE

How would you describe yourself to a stranger?

DAY FORTY

What are you most worried about right now? How long have you been worried about this?

DAY FORTY-ONE

Are you happy about how you spend your time? What would you change?

DAY FORTY-TWO

Write about a time you felt confident?

DAY FORTY-THREE

Write down five positive affirmations.

DAY FORTY-FOUR

Who are you most grateful for having in your life?

DAY FORTY-FIVE

During tough times, what helps you the most and why?

DAY FORTY-SIX

What is something that has bothered your recently?

DAY FORTY-SEVEN

Reflect on a past mistake.

DAY FORTY-EIGHT

Write down the positive ways you have changed over the past five or ten years?

DAY FORTY-NINE

What do you want more of in your life?

DAY FIFTY

Who can you reach out to today, some that always makes you feel good?

DAY FIFTY-ONE

What future plans do you have that you are looking forward to?

DAY FIFTY-TWO

What are the things that you need to stop doing that are making you unhappy?

DAY FIFTY-THREE

How can you be more kind to others?

DAY FIFTY-FOUR

Write about a time you were brave.

DAY FIFTY-FIVE

Who is someone you need to forgive?

DAY FIFTY-SIX

Are you living in a way that reflects the person you want to be?

DAY FIFTY-SEVEN

The ten biggest gifts you have to offer to the world.

DAY FIFTY-EIGHT

What does success mean to you?

DAY FIFTY-NINE

What do you think you need the most right now, and how can you meet that need?

DAY SIXTY

Do you care about what other people think about you? Why?

DAY SIXTY-ONE

Make a list of people with whom you have a good relationship and the reason why.

DAY SIXTY-TWO

What habits do you want to stop?

DAY SIXTY-THREE

How do you want people to remember you?

DAY SIXTY-FOUR

Write three things you like about your appearance.

DAY SIXTY-FIVE

Write a love letter to your body thanking it for carrying you and keeping you alive.

DAY SIXTY-SIX

What kind of person do you want to be for yourself and others today?

DAY SIXTY-SEVEN

List some challenges you have felt recently.

DAY SIXTY-EIGHT

Why are you a good friend?

DAY SIXTY-NINE

Describe yourself in ten words.

DAY SEVENTY

What do your family love about you?

DAY SEVENTY-ONE

List five places you want to travel and why?

DAY SEVENTY-TWO

What would you tell your past self?

DAY SEVENTY-THREE

What is your favourite hobby?

DAY SEVENTY-FOUR

Are you happy with your life? Why?

DAY SEVENTY-FIVE

If you could only keep three items you possess right now, what would they be and why?

DAY SEVENTY-SIX

What are your favourite ten songs?

DAY SEVENTY-SEVEN

When was the happiest time of your life? Why?

DAY SEVENTY-EIGHT

What makes you feel confident?

DAY SEVENTY-NINE

Where do you see yourself in a year?

DAY EIGHTY

What makes you feel loved?

DAY EIGHTY-ONE

Use this page to dump anything that's on your mind.

DAY EIGHTY-TWO

What are your priorities in life?

DAY EIGHTY-THREE

What are you passionate about?

DAY EIGHTY-FOUR

What are you currently struggling with?

DAY EIGHTY-FIVE

What does self-love mean to you?

DAY EIGHTY-SIX

What makes you feel peaceful?

DAY EIGHTY-SEVEN

What is your favourite childhood memory?

DAY EIGHTY-EIGHT

What five things are you grateful for?

DAY EIGHTY-NINE

What is your favourite thing about your personality?

DAY NINETY

Write down your bucket list.

DAY NINETY-ONE

What have you achieved that you are proud of?

DAY NINETY-TWO

What does your dream life look like?

DAY NINETY-THREE

How would your best friend describe you?

DAY NINETY-FOUR

List five of life's simple pleasures that you are grateful for.

DAY NINETY-FIVE

Why do you think self-worth is important?

DAY NINETY-SIX

How can you make tomorrow better?

DAY NINETY-SEVEN

List fifteen things that put a smile on your face.

DAY NINETY-EIGHT

What are your favourite TV Shows?

DAY NINETY-NINE

What is something you need to forgive yourself for?

DAY ONE HUNDRED

What made you last laugh?

AND LASTLY...

Use this space to reflect on your 100 days of journaling and what you have learnt.

WWW.LOVENDU.CO.UK
INSTAGRAM: @LOVENDU_
TWITTER: @LOVENDU_
PINTEREST: @LOVENDU_
FACEBOOK: @LOVENDUOFFICIAL

Printed in Great Britain
by Amazon